Complete Instant Pot Cookbook for Two

Easy, Healthy and Fast Instant Pot Pressure Cooker Recipes That Will Blow
Your Mind with Pictures and Nutrition Facts

Dave Pine© 2019

D1254742

Table of Contents

INTRODUCTION

The instant pot is an invention that has made the lives of others incredibly easy, and it's perfect for couples too! This instant pot cookbook has each and every recipe fit for two people so that eating delicious, healthy meals has never been easier. You can use the instant pot for any meal of the day from breakfast to dessert. You can even cook delicious side dishes to go with left over meat whenever you want or to finish the perfect dinner. You don't have to cook for a large family to use the instant pot to your advantage. Retire your old way of cooking, and allow the instant pot to help you cook healthy even with your busy day to day schedule. There's a little something for everyone, so just pick a recipe to get started.

USING THE INSTANT

In this chapter, we'll talk about how you use your instant pot for successful, tasty recipes.

WHEN BROWNING THINGS

You'll use your sauté function which will sear and brown meats. This will give your meat flavor because it seals in moisture. Leave your lid off when you sauté anything.

WHEN LOADING IT UP

You need to put the harder vegetables on the bottom, and then add the meat. The softer vegetables should go on top. Top with the liquid last, but never fill your pot more than two thirds full.

WHEN ADDING LIQUID

This is for when you're using the instant pot as a pressure cooker, which you will in all of these recipes. A cup of liquid will be needed for most recipes. However, if a recipe calls for less it's because the rest of the ingredients will make up for the missing liquid.

WHEN REDUCING

If you're trying to make a rich sauce, you will need to press the sauté function to reduce liquid, such as wine. This will cause the alcohol to evaporate but the wine flavor will still be there to add to the richness of your dish.

THE BUTTONS

Let's take a quick look at the buttons on your instant pot. These are usually the same for every instant pot, but if you have individual questions, check your instant pot's manual.

- **Manual:** This will let you to set the mode and time.
- **+ and -:** This is what you use to decrease and increase cooking time.
- **Pressure:** Switch from low to high depending on your recipe.
- **Adjust:** This will help you to adjust the pre-set times of your instant pot. So, if you're told to click the stew setting but need it set to only ten minutes, you'd use this button.
- **Keep Warm/Cancel:** You use this when switching between cooking and sauté. It can also be used to keep your food warm.
- **Slow Cook:** Your instant pot can serve as a slow cooker when you use this setting.

- **Steam:** Your instant pot serves as a steamer with this setting.
- **Yogurt:** This setting is usually only used to make yogurts, but it will also let you make porridges or pasteurize milk.
- **Rice:** This allows you to use your instant pot as a rice cooker. It automatically sets it to low, but you can change this if needed.
- **Bean/Chili:** The default for this setting is a half hour.
- **Meat/Stew:** The default for this is thirty-five minutes.
- **Porridge:** The name says it all with this one. Use it to make the perfect porridge.
- **Soup/Broth:** The default setting is a half hour.
- **Sauté:** The default setting is a half hour, so you'll need to cancel when you're done or extend the time as needed.

BREAKFAST RECIPES

CRANBERRY OATMEAL

Serves: 2
Time: 40 Minutes

Ingredients:

- 1 Tablespoon Butter, Unsalted
- ½ Cup Steel Cut Oats
- 2 Teaspoons Sugar
- Pinch Sea Salt
- 1 Cup Water
- ½ Cup Whole Milk
- ¼ Cup Cranberries, Dried
- ¼ Teaspoon Vanilla Extract, Pure
- ¼ Cup Almonds, Toasted & Chopped

Directions:

1. Start by pressing sauté, and make sure it's on medium heat. Melt your butter, and stir in your oats. Make sure the oats are well coated, and cook for three minutes. They

should become fragrant with a nutty aroma.

2. Add in your water, milk, sugar, salt, cranberries and vanilla. Stir well.

3. Lock the lid, and then cook on high pressure for ten minutes.

4. Allow for a natural pressure release for ten minutes before using a quick release next. Unlock the lid, and then spoon your oatmeal out. Top with almonds before serving. You can add in extra milk or sugar depending on your preference.

SIMPLE EGG MUFFINS

Serves: 2
Time: 40 Minutes

Ingredients:

- 2 Eggs
- ¼ Teaspoon Lemon Pepper Seasoning
- 2 Tablespoons Cheddar Cheese
- ½ Green Onion, Sliced
- Black Pepper to Taste
- 2 Slices Bacon

Directions:

1. Start by putting the steamer basket in the pot, and add in a cup and a half of water.
2. Put your eggs in a bowl and add in your lemon seasoning. Beat until well mixed.
3. Add in the bacon, cheese and green onion into two muffin cups, and then pour in the egg mixture.
4. Stir until combined, and put them on your steamer basket.
5. Lock the lid, and cook on high pressure for eight minutes. Use a quick release.
6. Serve warm.

OATMEAL GINGER MUFFINS

Serves: 2
Time: 45 Minutes

Ingredients:

- ½ Teaspoon Vanilla Extract, Pure
- 1/3 Cup Quick Oats
- 3 Tablespoons Butter, Unsalted & Melted
- ¼ Cup Brown Sugar
- 1 Egg
- ¼ Cup Greek Yogurt, Plain
- ½ Teaspoon Baking Powder
- ¼ Teaspoon Baking Soda
- ½ Teaspoon Cinnamon
- ½ Teaspoon Ground Ginger
- ½ Cup All Purpose Flour
- Pinch Sea Salt

- 2 Tablespoons Crystalized Ginger, Chopped Fine
- Nonstick Cooking Spray

Directions:

1. Get out a bowl and mix your brown sugar, butter, vanilla, egg and yogurt together. Get out a different bowl and mix your oats, flour, baking soda, baking powder, cinnamon, salt and ginger. Add your dry and wet ingredients together. Stir well.

2. Stir your ginger in, and then get out four ramekins. You can also use custard cups. Spray with coking spray generously, and then fill them three quarters full. Cover with foil, and then add a cup of water into your instant pot.

3. Put your trivet in, and then put the cups on top. Lock the lid, and cook on high pressure for twelve minutes. Use a natural pressure release for ten full minutes before using a quick release.

4. Unlock the lid, and remove your foil. Allow to cool before serving.

CLASSIC EGG BAKE

Serves: 2
Time: 15 Minutes

Ingredients:

- 2 Tablespoons Cheddar Cheese, Shredded
- 1 Cup Spinach, Torn
- 3 Eggs
- ½ Cup Hash browns
- 2 Slices Bacon, Chopped, Cooked & Crisp
- ¼ Cup Whole Milk
- Black Pepper to Taste

Directions:

1. Press sauté, and then add in your hash browns. Cook for two minutes before adding in the spinach.
2. Ge tout a bowl and mix your milk, cheese, and eggs. Add in your pepper, and whisk well. Pour it into the instant pot.
3. Seal the lid, and cook for five minutes on high pressure before using a quick release.
4. Serve with extra cheese.

APPLE FRENCH TOAST CUPS

Serves: 2

Time: 35 Minutes

Ingredients:

- 2 Tablespoons Heavy Whipping Cream

- 1 Egg

- ½ Cup while Milk

- ¼ Teaspoon Vanilla Extract, Pure

- 2 Teaspoons Brown Sugar

- ¼ Teaspoon Ground Cinnamon

- Pinch Sea Salt

- 2 Cups Bread Cubes

- ½ Small Apple, Cored, Peele & Grated

Directions:

1. Coat two ramekins with cooking spray, and then get out a bowl.

2. Whisk your eggs well before adding in cream, vanilla, milk, cinnamon, salt, and brown

sugar. Add in the bread cubes, and stir until it's well coated.

3. Let it sit for three minutes. This will make the bread absorb some of the mixture, and then add in the apple. Stir gently, and spoon this mixture into the cups, and then cover with foil.

4. Add a cup of water to your instant pot before adding in your trivet. Lock the lid, and cook on high pressure for eight minutes. Allow for a natural pressure release for five minutes before suing a quick release to finish.

5. Serve once cooled slightly.

EGG & SPINACH CONGEE

Serves: 2
Time: 50 Minutes

Ingredients:

- 2 Scallions, Sliced
- 2/3 Cup Arborio Rice
- 2 Teaspoons Ginger, Fresh & Minced
- 2 Cloves Garlic, Minced
- 2 Tablespoons Soy Sauce
- 1/8 Teaspoon Red Pepper Flakes
- 1 Teaspoon Rice Vinegar
- 4 Cups Vegetable Stock, Low Sodium
- 3 Cups Baby Spinach
- 2 Eggs, Beaten

Directions:

1. Throw your rice into your instant pot before adding in the white scallion parts, garlic, ginger, red pepper flakes, vinegar, stock and soy sauce.

2. Close the lid and lock it.

3. Cook on high pressure for twenty minutes, and then use a natural pressure release for ten minutes before using a quick release. Unlock the lid, and then add in your scallion greens and spinach. Stir well and allow them to wilt.

4. Drizzle in your beaten eggs, and then stir well. Whisk until you have threads of egg cooked in your broth. Allow it to thicken before serving warm.

SCOTCH EGGS

Serves: 2
Time: 15 Minutes

Ingredients:

- 1 Tablespoon Coconut Oil
- ½ lb. Ground Sausage
- 2 Eggs
- 2 Cups Water, Divided

Directions:

1. Start by putting a steamer basket in your instant pot and add your water and eggs. Secure the lid, and cook on high pressure for six minutes.

2. Allow for a natural pressure release and then submerse them in a bowl of cold water. Remove the shells when they're cool, and then divide your sausage in half. Flatten it with a spatula, and wrap your sausage patty around your egg.

3. Drain the instant pot, and add in your oi. Press sauté, and once it's heated, brown the sausage.

4. Remove the eggs, and then put the remaining cup of water in your instant pot. Add in your pan insert with the eggs on top. Seal the lid, and cook on high pressure for six minutes. Use a quick release and serve warm.

BROCCOLI & EGG BAKE

Serves: 2

Time: 10 Minutes

Ingredients:

- 3 Eggs, Whisked
- ¼ Teaspoon Garlic Powder
- ½ Cup Broccoli Florets
- 2 Tablespoons Tomatoes
- 1 Clove Garlic, Minced
- ½ Cup Red Bell Pepper, Chopped
- ½ Cup Yellow Onion, Chopped
- ¼ Teaspoon Chili Powder
- 2 Tablespoons Grated Cheese
- 2 Tablespoons Parsley, Fresh & Chopped
- 2 Tablespoons Onions, Chopped
- Sea Salt & Black Pepper to Taste

Directions:

1. Open the lid, and then grease the inside of your instant pot.

2. Get out a bowl and whisk your eggs, adding in all of your remaining ingredients except for the cheese. Season with slat and pepper. Seal the lid, and press steam. Cook for five minutes.

3. Use a quick release, and then serve topped with cheese.

BROCCOLI FRITTATA

Serves: 2
Time: 30 Minutes

Ingredients:

- 1 Cup Goats Milk
- 4 Eggs
- 1 Cup Goat Cheese, Shredded
- 8 Ounces Ham, Cubed
- 2 Cups Broccoli Florets, Frozen
- Sea Salt & Black Pepper to Taste

Directions:

1. Get out a baking pan that will fit in your instant pot and spray it. arrange your ham and broccoli at the bottom.
2. Get out a bowl and beat your milk and eggs together. Season with salt and pepper, and then mix in your cheese.
3. Pour the mixture over your ham, and then cover with foil.
4. Pour two cups of water into your instant pot and add in your trivet. Put the pan on it, and close the lid.
5. Cook on high pressure for twenty minutes and then use a quick release. Serve warm.

SPANISH TORTILLA

Serves: 2
Time: 40 Minutes

Ingredients:

- ¼ Cup Onion, Chopped
- 2 Tablespoons Olive Oil
- 1 Cup Hash browns, Frozen & Thawed
- 4 Eggs, Large
- 1 Teaspoon Sea Salt, Divided
- 1 Tablespoon Whole Milk
- 1 Teaspoon Smoked Paprika

Directions:

1. Spray a six-inch baking pan with cooking spray. Press sauté, and then add in the olive oil into your instant pot.

2. Add in your onion, and cook for four minutes. Add in your hash browns and season with salt. Cook for a minute. Spoon this mixture into your baking pan, and then rinse your inner pot out. Scrape any brown bits away.

3. Get out a bowl and whisk the eggs, and then whisk your paprika, milk and a pinch of salt. Pour it over your potato mixture.

4. Add a cup of water to your instant pot, and then add in the trivet with the pan on top. Cover your pan with foil, and lock the lid. Pre ss steam, and cook on high pressure for seven minutes. Allow for a natural pressure release for eight minutes before finishing with a quick release.

5. Unlock your lid, and then allow it to cool for three minutes before slicing to serve.

CHORIZO CASSEROLE

Serves: 2
Time: 45 Minutes

Ingredients:

- ½ lb. Chorizo, Casing Removed

- 3 Eggs, Large

- ½ Teaspoon Sea Salt

- ¾ Cup Whole Milk

- 2 Cups Stale Bread Cubes, Chopped into 1 Inch Pieces

- 4 Ounces Green Chilies, Canned, Drained & Rinsed

- ½ Cup Monterey Jack Cheese, Shredded

Directions:

1. Press sauté and adjust to medium heat, cooking your chorizo. Break it up into bite size pieces, and stir until browned. Remove your sausage and set it to the side. Rinse your inner pot out, making sure there is nothing left in it.

2. Get out a bowl and whisk your eggs before adding in your milk and salt. Add in the

21

bread cubes, and make sure they're coated. Allow them to sit for three minutes.

3. Stir once more before adding in your cheese, chorizo and green chilies. Stir again.

4. Coat the bottom of a one-quart baking dish that will fit in your instant pot with cooking spray. Add in your bread mixture and put foil on top. Do not crimp it.

5. Add a cup of water into the instant pot before putting your trivet in it. use the steam button and cook on high for twelve minutes before using a pressure release for ten minutes. Finish with a quick release, and allow it to cool for three minutes before serving.

TOMATO & BASIL QUICHE

Serves: 2
Time: 40 Minutes

Ingredients:

- ¾ Teaspoon Sea Salt, Divided
- 2 Eggs, Large
- 1 Tomato, Seeded & Diced
- 1/3 Cup Whole Milk
- 1/3 Cup Heavy Whipping Cream
- 1/8 Teaspoon Black Pepper
- 1 ¼ Cups Mozzarella, Grated
- 2 Tablespoons Basil, Fresh & Chopped

Directions:

1. Start by getting out a strainer and placing it on a bowl. Toss your diced tomatoes and a quarter teaspoon of salt on it, allowing it to drain.

2. Get out another bowl and whisk your eggs until they're completely mixed. Add in a half a teaspoon of salt, and mix again.

3. Get out a one quart baking dish, coating it in cooking spray. Sprinkle in half of your cheese on the bottom, topping with the basil and tomatoes. Add in the remaining cheese, pouring your egg mixture over it. cover with foil, but do not crimp it. your quiche will expand as it finishes cooking.

4. Pour a cup of water into your instant pot, and then put a trivet on the pot. Put a trivet in, and place the trivet on top.

5. Lock the lid, and select steam. Cook on high pressure for ten minutes before using a natural release for ten minutes. Finish with a quick release, and allow your quiche to cool for ten minutes before slicing to serve.

SAVORY EGG CUPS

Serves: 2
Time: 35 Minutes

Ingredients:

- 2 Eggs, Large
- ¼ Cup Ricotta Cheese
- 2 Tablespoons Sour Cream
- ¼ Teaspoon Sea Salt
- ¼ Teaspoon Dijon Mustard
- Pinch Black Pepper
- ¼ Cup Swiss Cheese, Grated
- 1 Ounce Ham, Chopped

Directions:

1. Get out a bowl and mix your eggs, sour cream, mustard, salt, pepper, and ricotta. Beat until there is no clumping.

2. Get out two ramekins, spraying them down generously with cooking spray. Place a

tablespoon of your Gruyere cheese on the bottom of each and then top with ham. Pour your egg mixture in next, and then sprinkle on the remaining cheese. Cover with foil, but don't crimp the sides. It needs room to expand.

3. Pour a cup of water into your instant pot, and put the trivet inside. Put the ramekins on top, and lock your lid. Cook on high pressure for seven minutes, and allow for a natural pressure release for a full five minutes. Fish with a quick release.

4. Allow them to cool before serving.

BREAKFAST CHICKEN CONGEE

Serves: 2
Time: 1 Hour 10 Minutes

Ingredients:

- 7 Cups Water
- 1 lb. Chicken Thighs
- 1 ½ Cups Shiitake Mushrooms
- ½ Inch Ginger, Peeled & Sliced
- 1 Cup Jasmine Rice, Uncooked
- 1 Clove Garlic
- ½ Tablespoon Soy Sauce
- ½ Tablespoon Toasted Sesame Oil
- 4 Tablespoons Peanuts
- ¼ Cup Cilantro, Fresh
- ½ Green Onion, Sliced
- 1 Egg, Boiled

Directions:

1. Start by crushing your garlic, and peel and slice your ginger. Slice your mushrooms

next, making sure you're slicing them into thin strips.

2. Trim your chicken, and then layer your rice on the bottom of the pot. Add I your ginger, mushrooms and garlic next. Put your chicken on top.

3. Pour in seven cups of water, and then lock the lid.

4. Cook on porridge mode, and then allow for a natural pressure release.

5. Remove your chicken, and shred them before putting it into the pot again.

6. Store again, and add salt as needed.

7. Serve drizzled with soy sauce, sesame oil, and then sprinkle with cilantro, peanuts and green onions.

LUNCH RECIPES

SALMON & GREENS

Serves: 2
Time: 25 Minutes

Ingredients:

- ½ Cloves Garlic, Chopped Fine

- ½ Tablespoon Lemon juice, Fresh

- ½ Tablespoon Rosemary, Fresh & Chopped

- Sea Salt & black Pepper to Taste

- 1 ½ Tablespoons Olive Oil

- ½ lb. Spinach, Fresh & Torn

- ½ lb. Salmon Fillets, Boneless

Directions:

1. Grease your instant pot with a tablespoon of olive oil, and then put the fillets in. season with rosemary, salt and pepper.

2. Drizzle the lemon juice over it with a half a cup of water. Close the lid, and cook on

high pressure for four minutes.

3. Use a quick release, and then get out a pot. Add your spinach and cover with water. Boil for three minutes. Drain it in a colander, and then take the salmon from the instant pot, placing the spinach at the bottom with the salmon on top.

4. Pour in a half a cup of water and garlic. Sauté for eight minutes before serving warm.

SHRIMP CREOLE

Serves: 2
Time: 20 Minutes

Ingredients:

- 1 Clove Garlic, Minced
- 1 Celery Stalk, Diced
- ½ lb. Jumbo Shrimp, Peeled & Deveined
- 1 Teaspoon Olive Oil
- ½ Teaspoon Thyme
- ½ Onion, Diced
- 14 Ounces Tomatoes, Canned & Diced
- ½ Bell Pepper, Diced

Directions:

1. Press sauté, and heat up your oil.
2. Stir the garlic, celery and onion in. cook for three minutes before tossing the remaining ingredients in. stir well.
3. Cook on high pressure for a minute, and then use a quick release. Press sauté, and reduce the liquid for ten minutes before serving warm.

SALMON & BROCCOLI

Serves: 2
Time: 5 Minutes

Ingredients:

- Sea Salt & Black Pepper to Taste
- 1 Cup Water
- 2 Salmon Fillets
- ½ Teaspoon Garlic Powder
- 5 Ounces Broccoli Florets

Directions:

1. Start by seasoning the fillets with salt, pepper and garlic.
2. Sprinkle your broccoli with salt and pepper, and then pour the water into the instant pot. Arrange the salmon in a steamer basket, and scatter the broccoli around it.
3. Seal and cook on high pressure for two minutes.
4. Use a quick release, and serve warm.

PORK CHILI

Serves: 2
Time: 55 Minutes

Ingredients:

- ½ Onion, Chopped
- ½ Teaspoon Ground Cumin
- 1 ½ Cups Beef Broth
- 1 Clove Garlic, Crushed
- ½ lb. Pork Shoulder
- 3 New Mexico Chilies, Halved & Seeded

Directions:

1. Start by getting out a saucepan, and toss your garlic, onion and chilies together.
2. Pour 1 ½ cups of water into the saucepan, bringing it to a boil. Once it's boiled, allow it to cool for fifteen minutes.
3. Take this mixture and place it in a blender, blending until smooth.
4. Put your pork in the instant pot adding the mixture and beef broth. Select the m eat button, cooking for thirty minutes.
5. Use a natural release for ten minutes before serving warm.

TURKEY VERDE CASSEROLE

Serves: 2
Time: 35 Minutes

Ingredients:

- ½ Cup Brown Rice
- ½ Onion, Sliced
- ¼ Cup Salsa Verde
- 1 lb. Turkey Tenderloins
- 1 Cup Chicken Broth
- Sea Salt to Taste

Directions:

1. Put all of your ingredients in the instant pot, and then seal it. cook on high pressure for eight minutes.
2. Allow for a natural pressure release for ten minutes before serving. If needed, use a quick release for any remaining pressure.

CLASSIC TURKEY CASSEROLE

Serves: 2
Time: 20 Minutes

Ingredients:

- ½ Cup Cherry Tomatoes, Halved

- ¼ Cup Kalamata Olives, Chopped

- ½ Cup Sour Cream

- ½ Cup Rice, Cooked

- ½ Zucchini, Shredded

- 1 Cup Turkey, Cooked & Shredded

- ¼ Cup Chicken Broth

- 1 Tablespoon Onion, Diced

- 1 Clove Garlic, Minced

- ½ Tablespoon Butter

Directions:

1. Press sauté, and stir in your onions. Cook for tow minutes, and then add your garlic. Cook for a minute more.

2. Add your remaining ingredients and stir well.

3. Cook on high pressure for three minutes.

4. Use a quick release and serve warm.

CAJUN SHRIMP WITH ASPARAGUS

Serves: 2
Time: 25 Minutes

Ingredients:

- 1 ½ Cups Water
- ½ Teaspoon Olive Oil
- 12 Spears Asparagus, Trimmed
- ½ Teaspoon Olive Oil
- ½ lb. Shrimp, Peeled & deveined
- ½ Tablespoon Cajun Seasoning

Directions:

1. Pour the water into the instant pot, and put the asparagus on a rack. Put your shrimp on top. Drizzle with oil and Cajun seasoning.
2. Cook using steam for two minutes on low pressure.
3. Use a quick release and serve warm.

CLASSIC CARNITAS

Serves: 2
Time: 1 Hour 10 Minutes

Ingredients:

- 1 Bay Leaf
- 1 Clove Garlic, Slivered
- ¼ Teaspoon Oregano
- ¼ Teaspoons Garlic Powder
- ¼ Teaspoon Adobo Seasoning
- ½ Teaspoon Cumin
- 1 lb. Roast
- ¼ Cup Vegetable Broth, Low Sodium
- 1 Chipotle Pepper with Adobo Sauce

Directions:

1. Start by pressing sauté, and season the pork before placing it in your instant pot. Allow

it to cook on five minutes per side. Remove and allow it to cool.

2. Get a sharp knife and make a one-inch incision as deep as you can, and add in the garlic slivers.

3. Add any additional seasoning now, rubbing it in.

4. Place your bay leaf, chipotle pepper and broth in the instant pot, and then add the meat. Cook for fifty minutes on high pressure.

5. Use a quick release, and then shred your pork.

6. Return it to the instant pot so that it can soak some juices up before serving in tortillas with cheese if desired.

SPINACH & ARTICHOKE RISOTTO

Serves: 2
Time: 35 Minutes

Ingredients:

- ½ Onion, Small & Divided
- 2 Tablespoons Butter, Unsalted & Divided
- ½ Cup + 2 Tablespoon Arborio Rice
- ¼ Cup White Wine
- ½ Cup Artichoke Hearts, Canned & Drained
- 2 Cups Vegetable Stock, Low Sodium & Divided
- 2 Cups Baby Spinach
- ¼ Cup Parmesan, Grated
- ¼ Teaspoon Sea Salt

Directions:

1. Press sauté and put the heat to medium. Put a tablespoon of butter in, and then once it's hot add in your onion. Cook for three minutes. Add in your rice, and make sure it's coated in butter. Cook it for a minute before adding in the artichoke hearts. Stir, and then add in the wine. Cook for three minutes. Most of the wine should evaporate.

41

2. Add in 1 ¾ cup stock, and then add salt. Stir well before closing the lid. Cook on high pressure for eight minutes, and then use a quick release.

3. Check your risotto It should be firm at the center, and your sauce should be creamy. Add another ¼ cup of stock if it's done and add in your spinach. Press sauté, and then cook for three minutes. The spinach should wilt.

4. Stir in your remaining tablespoon of butter and cheese. If your rice is sticking, add a little more stock to loosen it up. Serve warm.

MUSHROOM STROGANOFF

Serves: 2
Time: 35 Minutes

Ingredients:

- ½ Cup Sherry, Dry

- 1 lb. Mushrooms, Sliced

- 1 Tablespoon Butter, Unsalted

- 2 ¼ Cups Mushroom Stock

- 1 Sea Salt

- 4 Ounces Egg Noodles

- ¼ Cup Sour Cream

- 2 Tablespoon Parsley, Fresh & Chopped to Garnish

Directions:

1. Press sauté, and then set the heat to medium. Place your butter in the instant pot, and add in your onion once it's hot. Cook for three minutes. Add in the mushroom, cooking for three minutes.

2. Pour in your sherry, and bring it to a simmer. Cook for three minutes, and the alcohol

should reduce by half. Add the salt, noodles and stock. Mix well.

3. Close and lock the lid. Cook on high pressure for five minutes before finishing with a quick release. Open the lid, letting it rest and then the sauce should begin to simmer and cool.

4. Once it's cooled slightly add in the sour cream and stir it in.

5. Garnish with parsley before serving.

SPICY TOFU & CARROTS

Serves: 2
Time: 25 Minutes

Ingredients:

- 8 Ounces Tofu, Firm & Cut into 1 Inch Cubes
- 2 Carrots, Cut into 1 Inch Chunks
- 1 Tablespoon Soy Sauce
- 1 Tablespoon Sugar
- 1 Scallion, Sliced Thin
- 2 Cloves Garlic, Minced
- 1 Teaspoon Red Pepper Flakes
- 1/3 Cup Water
- 1 Tablespoon Sesame Oil
- 1 Teaspoon Toasted Sesame Seeds

Directions:

1. Put your carrots and tofu in the instant pot before adding in your sugar, soy sauce, white scallion pars, red pepper flakes, water and garlic.
2. Close the lid, and cook on high pressure for four minutes. Sue a quick release.
3. Unlock the lid, and then stir in your sesame oil. Simmer for three minutes, and serve garnished with scallion greens and sesame seeds.

CHICKEN WITH SHIRATAKI NOODLES

Serves: 2

Time: 20 Minutes

Ingredients:

- ½ lb. Chicken Breasts, Grilled
- ½ Cup Coconut Milk
- ½ Cup Shirataki Noodles
- 4 Ounces Cheddar Cheese, Shredded
- 2 Cups Water
- Sea Salt & Black Pepper to Taste

Directions:

1. Add your water and noodles in first, and cook on high pressure for five minutes.
2. Use a quick release before pressing sauté. Add in the coconut milk and cheese, stirring until all of your cheese is melted.
3. Place with grilled chicken on top.

SPICY CHICKEN

Serves: 2
Time: 20 Minutes

Ingredients:

- 1 Jalapeno, Dice d& Seeded
- ¼ Teaspoon Paprika
- ½ Teaspoon Cumin
- Pinch Black Pepper
- ¼ Teaspoon Cumin
- 1/3 Teaspoon Onion Flakes
- ½ Teaspoon Garlic Powder
- ½ lb. Chicken Tenders

Directions:

1. Start by getting out a bowl and mix all of your seasonings together and use it to coat your chicken.

2. Seal the lid, and cook on your poultry setting for fifteen minutes. Use a quick release, and allow it to sit for five minutes before serving.

CLASSIC MINESTRONE

Serves: 2
Time: 30 Minutes

Ingredients:

- 3 Tablespoons Olive Oil
- 1 Carrot, Small & Diced
- ½ Onion, Small & Diced
- 1 Teaspoon Garlic, Minced
- ½ Zucchini, Diced
- 7 Ounces Diced Tomatoes, Canned
- 15 Ounces Cannellini Beans, Canned, Drained & Rinsed
- 1 ½ Cups Vegetable Stock, Low Sodium
- ½ Cup Elbow Macaroni
- 1 Bay Leaf
- 1 Teaspoon Italian Herb Blend
- ½ Teaspoon Oregano

- ½ Teaspoon Basil
- ½ Teaspoon Sea Salt
- ¼ Teaspoon Red Pepper Flakes
- 2 Cups Baby Spinach
- ¼ Cup Parmesan Cheese, Grated
- 3 Tablespoons Pesto

Directions:

1. Pres sauté, adjusting it to medium heat instead of high. Pour the olive oil in, and allow it to heat up. When it starts to shimmer add in your carrot, onion and garlic. Stir so it doesn't stick, cooking for about five minutes. Your vegetable should start to soften.

2. Add in the tomatoes, beans, stock, zucchini, bay leaf, Italian herbs, macaroni, salt, and red pepper flakes.

3. Lock the lid before setting it to high pressure for five minutes. Let it use a natural pressure release for two minutes before finishing with a quick release.

4. Remove the bay leaf, and stir in your spinach. Once it's wilted, top with parmesan and pesto before serving warm.

EASY RATATOUILLE

Serves: 2
Time: 30 Minutes

Ingredients:

- 1 Eggplant, Small & Sliced

- 2 Zucchini, Small & Sliced

- 6 Ounces Roasted Red Peppers, Canned & Sliced

- ½ Tablespoons Olive Oil

- ½ Onion, Sliced

- Sea Salt to Taste

- 1 Clove Garlic, Minced

- ¼ Cup Water

- 14 Ounces Crushed Tomatoes, Canned

Directions:

1. Press sauté, and then add your olive oil in. when it starts to shimmer add in all of your vegetables except for your tomatoes, sautéing for three minutes.

2. Pour in your tomatoes and water before seasoning with salt, and lock your lid. Cook on high pressure for four minutes.

3. Use a quick release, and serve cold as a side dish or hot over rice as a main course.

DINNER RECIPES

STEAK & VEGETABLES

Serves: 2
Time: 40 Minutes

Ingredients:

- ½ lb. Round Steak, Cubed

- 2 Bell Peppers, Chopped

- ½ Cup Mushrooms, Sliced

- 2 Potatoes, Cubed

- 1 Carrot, Peeled & Chopped

- 1 Tablespoon Flour

- 1 Tablespoon Butter

- ¼ Teaspoon Onion Powder

- ½ Teaspoon Garlic Salt

- 1 Cup Beef Broth

Directions:

1. Combine the steak with flour, and then melt your butter in the instant pot after pressing sauté. Brown the meat on both sides for three to five minutes per side. Add in remaining ingredients, and select meat/stew. Cook for thirty-five minutes.

2. Use a quick release and drain the liquid away before serving.

APPLE & CHERRY PORK

Serves: 2
Time: 45 Minutes

Ingredients:

- 1 Apple, Small & Diced
- 1/3 Cup Cherries, Pitted
- 3 Tablespoons Onion, Diced
- ¼ Cup Apple Juice
- 3 Tablespoons Celery, Diced
- ¾ lb. Pork Lion
- ¼ Cup Water
- Black Pepper to Taste

Directions:

1. Throw all the ingredients into the instant pot and mix well. Seal the lid, and choose the poultry setting. Cook for five minutes, before using a quick release.
2. Serve warm.

PORK CHOPS WITH CABBAGE

Serves: 2
Time: 25 Minutes

Ingredients:

- 2 Pork Chops

- ½ Teaspoon Fennel Seeds

- 1 Cabbage, Small

- 1 ½ Teaspoons Coconut Oil

- Black Pepper to Taste

- 1/3 Cup Beef Stock

- 1 ½ Teaspoons Coconut Oil

- 1 Teaspoon Almond Flour

Directions:

1. Start by pressing sauté, and then sprinkle the chops with fennel, salt and pepper. Slice your cabbage into slices that are ¾ inch thick. Place your cabbage to the side.

2. Put your oil int your instant pot, and press sauté. Once it's hot, add in your pork chops to brown on all sides.

3. Set your pork chops to the side, adding your cabbage in. place the pork chops on top before pouring the stock in.

4. Cook on high pressure for eight minutes, and then remove the meat. Tent with foil.

5. Allow it to come to a boil by pressing sauté, and stir in the flour. Pour the thickened sauce over your meat and cabbage to serve warm.

PORK GOULASH

Serves: 2
Time: 35 Minutes

Ingredients:

- ¼ lb. Pork Net, Chopped
- ¼ lb. Mushrooms
- 2 Cups Beef Broth
- 2 Tablespoons Vegetable Oil
- ½ Chili Pepper, Small & Sliced
- ½ Carrot, Chopped
- 1 Onion, Chopped
- ½ Stalk Celery, Chopped
- ½ Tablespoon Cayenne

Directions:

1. Oil your instant pot down and add in your onion. Fry for two minutes. Add in the carrot, celery, cayenne and chili powder. Cook for three more minutes and stir often to avoid burning or sticking.

2. Add your beef broth, meat, and mushrooms. Cook for thirty minutes on high pressure.

3. Use a quick release, and serve warm.

ROOT BEER PORK

Serves: 2
Time: 2
Time: 50 Minutes

Ingredients:

- 1 lb. Pork Roast
- Black Pepper to Taste
- 2/3 Cup Onion, Sliced
- 2 Tablespoons Ketchup
- 1/3 Cup Root Beer
- 1 ½ Teaspoons Almond Flour
- ¼ Teaspoon Lemon Juice, Fresh
- 1 ½ Teaspoons Worcestershire Sauce
- 1 Tablespoon Tomato Paste
- 1 ½ Teaspoons Honey, Raw

Directions:

1. Start by seasoning your pork roast using garlic, salt and pepper. Place the roast in the instant pot, and throw the rest of the ingredients in.
2. Press the meat/stew button, and then cook for thirty-five minutes.
3. Take the roast and onions out, discarding your onions. Shred the pork, and stir the pork back in.

TURKEY & MUSHROOMS

Serves: 2
Time: 5 Minutes

Ingredients:

- 1 lb. Turkey Breasts
- 1 Tablespoon Olive Oil
- ½ Teaspoon Thyme
- 3 Ounces Mushrooms, Sliced
- 1/3 Cup White Wine
- 1 Clove Garlic, Minced
- 1 ½ Tablespoons Heavy Cream
- 1 ½ Tablespoons Shallots, Chopped
- ½ Tablespoon Cornstarch
- 1/3 Cup Chicken Broth

Directions:

1. Tie the turkey crosswise two inches apart with kitchen twine.
2. Add your oil and press sauté, browning your turkey on all sides.
3. Place it on a plate, and in your instant pot throw in your shallots, mushrooms, garlic and thyme. Cook for three minutes. It should soften, and then add the turkey back in.
4. Pour in your white wine and broth, and then cook on high pressure for fifteen minutes before using a quick release. Switch your instant pot to sauté, and then put your turkey on a place. Untie it to slice, and then get out a pot.
5. In the pot whisk your heavy cream with cornstarch. Cook until thickened, and serve with sauce.

CREAM CHEESE & BACON CHICKEN

Serves: 2
Time: 40 Minutes

Ingredients:

- 4 Ounces Cream Cheese
- 1 Cup Water
- 1 lb. Chicken Breasts, Boneless & Skinless
- 2 Ounces Cheddar Cheese, Shredded
- ½ Ounce Ranch Seasoning
- 1 ½ Tablespoons Cornstarch
- 4 Bacon Slices, Cooked & Crumbled

Directions:

1. Start by mixing your ranch, water and cream cheese together before adding the chicken.
2. Cook on high pressure for twenty-five minutes before suing a quick release.
3. Remove the chicken, and then shred it.

4. Return to the pot, and then add your cheddar and bacon.

5. Press sauté, and cook for five minutes. S

6. Stir the cornstarch in, cooking for three more minutes or until thickened. Serve warm.

TOMATO & SOUR CREAM CHICKEN

Serves; 2

Time: 45 Minutes

Ingredients:

- 1 Cup Chicken Broth
- 2 Chicken Breasts, Boneless
- ½ Cup Sour Cream
- Sea Salt & Black Pepper to Taste
- 1/8 Teaspoon Garlic powder
- 7 Ounces Tomatoes, Canned & Diced

Directions:

1. Place your broth and chicken in the instant pot, and cook on high pressure for twenty minutes before using a quick release. Shred the chicken, and discard the cooking liquid. Press sauté, and stir in all remaining ingredients.

2. Cook for five minutes, and serve warm.

CLASSIC CHICKEN & POTATOES

Serves: 2
Time: 10 Minutes

Ingredients:

- 2 Potatoes, Wedges

- 1 Clove Garlic, Crushed

- ½ Tablespoon Lemon Juice

- 2 Chicken Thighs, Boneless

- ½ Teaspoon Mint, Fresh & Chopped

- 1 cup Water

- ¼ Tablespoon Cayenne

- ½ Teaspoon Ground Ginger

- 1/8 Teaspoon Olive Oil

- Sea Salt to Taste

Directions:

1. Start by getting out a bowl and mix your crushed garlic, lemon juice, olive oil, ginger, mint, cayenne and salt. Brush your chicken down with the mixture.

2. Grease your instant pot with what remains of the mix, and then add the potatoes and chicken. Add your water, and then select the meat setting. Cook for fifteen minutes.

3. Sue a natural release for ten minutes before finishing with a quick release.

MAPLE BRISKET

Serves: 2
Time: 55 Minutes

Ingredients:

- 1 lb. Beef Brisket
- 1 Tablespoon Maple Sugar
- Sea Salt & Black Pepper to Taste
- ½ Teaspoon Onion Powder
- ¼ Teaspoon Paprika
- ½ Teaspoon Mustard Powder
- 1 Cup beef Broth
- 1 ½ Teaspoons Liquid Smoke
- 2 Sprigs Thyme, Fresh

Directions:

1. Rub your brisket down with the dry spices, and then press sauté. Grease with oil, and brown your brisket.

2. Make sure the brisket has the fat side up, and then add your broth, liquid smoke and

thyme.

3. Cook on high pressure for forty minutes, and then allow for a natural pressure release. Remove your brisket, covering it with foil.

4. Press sauté, and then reduce the left-over liquid. Drizzle your brisket with the liquid before serving.

PORK CURRY

Serves: 2
Time: 30 Minutes

Ingredients:

- 2 Carrots, Sliced
- ¼ Teaspoon turmeric
- 1 ½ Tablespoons Garam Masala
- 4 Ounces Tomatoes, Diced
- 1 Tablespoon Ghee
- ¼ Zucchini, Diced
- Pinch Black Pepper
- ½ Cup Coconut Milk
- ½ Onion, Diced
- 1 Inch Piece ginger, Grated Fresh
- 2 Cloves Garlic, Minced
- ½ Lime, Juiced

- 1 lb. Pork

Directions:

1. Tart by putting your m eat in a sealable container. Add your coconut milk, lime juice, garlic and ginger. Mix well, and then allow it to marinate overnight.

2. Put your garam masala, ghee, onions, carrots, meat and tomatoes int the instant pot.

3. Cook on high pressure for twenty minutes, allowing a natural release for ten minutes. Use a quick release for remaining pressure, and then press sauté.

4. Add in your zucchini, simmering for five minutes. Serve warm over rice.

GARLIC & LEMON CHICKEN

Serves: 2
Time: 40 Minutes

Ingredients:

- 1 lb. Chicken Breasts

- 1 Onion, Diced

- ½ Tablespoon Butter

- ¼ Cup Chicken Broth

- 1 Clove Garlic, Minced

- ½ Teaspoon Parsley, Dried

- ¼ Teaspoon Paprika

- Dash White Wine

- ½ Lemon, Juiced

- 2 Teaspoons Arrowroot Powder

Directions:

1. Press sauté and add your butter and onion. Cook until softened and browned. This should take roughly ten minutes. Combine your remaining ingredients except for the flour. Cover, and then select poultry seasoning.

2. Use a quick release.

3. Thicken up the sauce with a slurry made of ¼ cup of sauce and flour. Mix it into the pot, and allow it to thicken and rest.

4. Stir well and serve warm.

HONEY BOURBON CHICKEN

Serves: 2
Time: 40 Minutes

Ingredients:

- ¼ Cup Onion, Diced

- 2 Tablespoons Ketchup

- ¼ Cup Soy Sauce

- ½ Cup Honey, Raw

- 1 Tablespoon Coconut Oil

- 1 Teaspoon Garlic, Minced

- Dash Red Pepper Flakes

- Dash Black Pepper

- ¾ lb. Chicken Breasts

- 1 Tablespoon Cornstarch

- 1 ½ Teaspoons Water

Directions:

1. Tart by placing everything but your cornstarch and water into your instant pot. Seal the lid, and cook for fifteen minutes on high pressure.

2. Use a quick release, and then shred the chicken.

3. Press sauté, and mix your water and cornstarch together to create a slurry. Add it into your liquid, cooking for a few minutes. It should thicken, and add your chicken back in.

4. Mix well before serving warm.

SPICY THIGHS

Serves: 2
Time: 30 Minutes

Ingredients:

- 1 Cup Chicken Stock
- ½ Tablespoon Vinegar
- ½ Tablespoon Soy Sauce
- 2 Cloves Garlic, Minced
- 2 ½ Tablespoons Chili Sauce
- 2 ½ Tablespoons Hoisin Sauce
- 1 Chicken Thighs, Boneless

Directions:

1. Start by putting your chicken in, and then whisk all remaining ingredients together before pouring it in.
2. Cook on high pressure for fifteen minutes, and then allow for a natural pressure release for fifteen minutes. Finish off with a quick release if needed.

KOREAN BEEF

Serves: 2

Time: 1 Hour

Ingredients:

- ½ Orange, Juiced
- 1 Tablespoon Ginger, Grated Fresh
- 2 Cloves Garlic, Minced
- Dash Soy Sauce, Low Sodium
- ¾ Cup Beef Broth
- 2 Tablespoons Olive Oil
- Sea Salt & Black Pepper to Taste
- 1 Apple Slice, Chopped & Peeled
- 1 lb. Bottom Beef Roast, Cubed

Directions:

1. Season your roast if desired, and then press sauté. Add your oil in, and once it shimmers add in your beef roast. Let it brown, and then use the broth to deglaze the pan. Add the soy sauce and mix well. Return the meat to your pan, and top with apple, ginger, garlic and orange juice. Stir well.

2. Seal the lid, and cook on high pressure for forty-five minutes.

3. Use a quick release, and let it cool slightly before shredding. Top with liquid before serving over rice.

SWEET SRIRACHA CHICKEN

Serves: 2

Time: 15 Minutes

Ingredients:

- 4 Tablespoons Water, Divided
- 1 ½ Tablespoons Sriracha
- 2 ½ Tablespoons Soy Sauce
- 1 ½ Tablespoons Honey, Raw
- 1 Tablespoon Cornstarch
- ½ Tablespoon Garlic, Minced
- 1 Teaspoon Sugar
- 2 Chicken Breasts, Diced

Directions:

1. Combine a tablespoon of water with sriracha, honey, soy sauce, garlic and sugar. Pour

it into your instant pot and add your chicken. Stir well.

2. Cook on high pressure for nine minutes, and use a quick release.

3. Whisk your remaining water with cornstarch before adding it. cook on sauté for three minutes so that it thickens before serving.

SPICY POT ROAST

Serves: 2
Time: 2 Hours

Ingredients:

- Sea Salt & Black Pepper to Taste
- 1 Packet Gravy Mix
- 1 Packet Ranch Dressing
- ½ Pepperoncini Juice
- 2 Whole Pepperoncini
- ¼ Stick Butter, Unsalted
- 1 lb. Roast
- ¼ Cup Beef Broth, Low Sodium

Directions:

1. Start by adding your juice and broth, and then add in your roast, gravy, and ranch mix. Make sure it's coated. Top with pepperoncini and butter.
2. Seal your instant pot, and cook on high pressure for ninety minutes.
3. Use a natural pressure release for fifteen minutes before finishing with a quick release.

CHICKEN ALFREDO

Serves: 2
Time: 30 Minutes

Ingredients:

- 4 Ounces Cream Cheese
- ¼ Cup Butter
- 1 Cup Cauliflower Florets
- 1 Cup Heavy Cream
- 2 Cloves Garlic, Chopped
- 2 Basil Leaves, Fresh & Chopped
- 2 Chicken Breasts, Boneless, Skinless & Chopped

Directions:

1. Press sauté, and then melt the butter. Whisk in your cream cheese before whisking in the heavy cream.
2. Add your remaining ingredients, and stir well.
3. Seal the lid, and cook on high pressure for fifteen minutes.
4. Use a quick release, and serve immediately.

SPICY CHICKEN & POTATOES

Serves: 2
Time: 35 Minutes

Ingredients:

- ½ Onion, Diced
- 1 ½ Tablespoon Buffalo Wing Sauce
- 8 Ounces Potatoes, Diced
- ¼ Teaspoon Garlic Powder
- 1 Cup Chicken Broth
- ½ lb. Chicken Breasts, Cubed
- Sea Salt & Black Pepper to Taste
- 1 ½ Tablespoon Butter, Divided

Directions:

1. Melt a half a tablespoon of butter in your instant pot after pressing sauté. Add the onion in, and cook for four minutes.
2. Stir the remaining ingredients in and press the poultry setting. Cook for eighteen minutes before using a quick release to serve warm.

CLASSIC STEAK

Serves: 2

Time: 50 Minutes

Ingredients:

- 1 ½ Teaspoons Worcestershire Sauce
- 1 lb. Flank Steak
- 2 Tablespoons Apple Cider Vinegar
- ¼ Cup Olive Oil
- 1 Tablespoon Onion Soup Mix

Directions:

1. Press sauté, and brown your steak on both sides.
2. Add in your onion soup mix, olive oil, vinegar and Worcestershire. Lock your lid.
3. Cook for thirty-five minutes on meat/stew setting. Use a quick release and serve warm.

KETCHUP & HONEY CHICKEN

Serves: 2
Time: 45 Minutes

Ingredients:

- 1 Teaspoon Garlic Powder
- 1/8 Cup Butter
- 1/8 Cup Coconut Aminos
- Sea Salt & Black Pepper to Taste
- 2 Chicken Thighs, Boneless
- 1/8 Cup Honey, Raw
- 1 ½ Tablespoons Ketchup

Directions:

1. Put everything in the instant pot, and stir well.
2. Cook on high pressure for eighteen minutes, and then use a quick release.
3. Press sauté, and cook for five more minutes before serving warm.

TURMERIC CHICKEN THIGHS

Serves: 2

Time: 20 Minutes

Ingredients:

- ½ Cup Water

- 1 Tablespoon Hot Sauce

- 1 Tablespoon Black Molasses

- 2 Tablespoons Coconut Oil

- ½ Tablespoon Lemon Juice, Fresh

- ¼ Cup Honey, Raw

- ½ Teaspoon Turmeric

- ½ Teaspoon Cumin

- ½ Teaspoon Coriander

- ½ Teaspoon Ginger

- 1 lb. Chicken Thighs

Directions:

1. Combine your spices in a bowl, and then coat your chicken in them. Put your coconut oil in the instant pot, and press sauté. Brown the chicken thighs evenly. Remove them, and then add the water. Allow it to come to a quick boil and then remove the browned bits before returning the chicken to the instant pot.

2. Cook on high pressure for fifteen minutes.

3. Combine your honey, lemon and molasses in a bowl together while your chicken cooks.

4. Use a quick release, and then remove the chicken, covering it in foil. This will help it to keep warm. Press sauté, and then add in your honey mixture. Let it boil, and whisk well. Cook until your sauce thickens, and dip your thighs in the sauce before serving.

EASY TERIYAKI CHICKEN

Serves: 2
Time: 30 Minutes

Ingredients:

- 1/3 Teaspoon Ginger
- 1 Clove Garlic, Crushed
- ¼ Cup Honey, Raw
- 1 Tablespoon Cornstarch
- ¼ Cup Water
- ¼ Onion, Sliced
- ¼ Cup Soy Sauce, Low Sodium
- ¼ Cup Rice Vinegar
- Pinch Black Pepper
- 2 Chicken Breasts

Directions:

1. Start by coating your instant pot with cooking spray, and then put your chicken in first.

2. Get out a bowl and mix your garlic, rice vinegar, onion, and remaining seasoning. Mix well. Add your soy sauce and honey, mixing again.

3. Coat your chicken in the mixture, and then cook on high pressure for fifteen minutes. Use a quick release, and take the chicken out to shred it.

4. Get out a different bowl and combine your cornstarch and water to make a slurry. Add it into your instant pot, and press sauté. Whisk well and allow it to sauté for sixty seconds to thicken. It should come to a boil.

5. Turn it off, and then add your chicken back in. serve over rice.

CHEESY CHICKEN

Serves: 2

Time: 40 Minutes

Ingredients:

- 2 Ounces Cream Cheese

- 2 Ounces cheddar Cheese

- 1 lb. Chicken Breast

- 2 Slices Bacon

- 1 Cup Water

- Sea Salt & Black Pepper to Taste

- 1 Packet Ranch Seasoning

- 1 ½ Tablespoons Cornstarch

Directions:

1. Press sauté, and then cook your bacon until it's crisp and will crumble easily.

2. Place your chicken in next, topping with cream cheese and seasoning. Pour in a cup of water, and cook on high pressure for twenty-five minutes.

3. Select a quick release, and then shred your chicken, but don't return it to the instant pot yet.

4. Turn the heat to low, and whisk your cornstarch in before returning your chicken to the instant pot. Add in your bacon and cheese, mixing well before serving.

SIDE DISHES

LEMON ARTICHOKES

Serves: 2
Time: 40 Minutes

Ingredients:

- 2 Artichokes
- ½ Lemon, Juiced
- ½ Lemon, Sliced into Wedges
- 1 ½ Cups Water
- 1 Tablespoon Dijon Mustard

Directions:

1. Trim your artichokes, and then rub the lemon wedge over the cuts. Add a cup and a half of water to your instant pot, and then put your steamer basket in. place the artichokes on top, and drizzle with lemon juice.

2. Cook for twenty minutes on high pressure, and then allow a natural release for ten minutes before finishing with a quick release. Season with salt and pepper.

3. Drizzle with Dijon before serving warm.

STUFFED EGGPLANT

Serves: 2
Time: 50 Minutes

Ingredients:

- ½ Cup Celery, Diced
- ½ Onion, Diced
- ½ Tablespoon Basil
- ½ Tablespoon Olive Oil
- 1 Cup Water
- 1 Cup Cheddar Cheese, Grated
- ½ lb. Mushrooms, Chopped
- 2 Eggplants

Directions:

1. Slice the eggplants in half, and then scoop the flesh out. Keep the hollowed eggplants for later.

2. Pour the water into the instant pot, and then combine your eggplant flesh with the remaining ingredients except for your cheese. Put this mixture into the instant pot with

your cooking liquid. Cook on high pressure for five minutes, and then use a natural release for ten minutes. Open and divide the filling between your eggplants, and then drizzle with olive oil on a rack. Sprinkle with salt and pepper. Do not remove the cooking liquid from your instant pot.

3. Cook on high pressure for fifteen minutes.

4. Use a quick release, sprinkle with cheese, and then close the lid again. Cook on high pressure for five more minutes before finishing with a quick release. Serve warm.

SESAME BOK CHOY

Serves: 2
Time: 5 Minutes

Ingredients:

- 1 Cup Water
- ½ Teaspoon Soy Sauce
- ¼ Teaspoon Sesame Oil
- 1 Teaspoon Sesame Seeds
- ½ Bok Choy

Directions:

1. Add the water to your instant pot before adding in your basket with the bok choy on top. Close the lid, cooking on high for four minutes.
2. Use a quick release, and then chop your bok choy. Drizzle with oil and soy sauce. Sprinkle with sesame seeds before serving.

SPICY SPINACH & EGGPLANT

Serves: 2
Time: 15 Minutes

Ingredients:

- ½ Tablespoon Five Spice Powder
- 1 Cup Spinach, Torn
- ½ Teaspoon Chili Powder
- ¼ Cup Coconut Milk
- ½ Cup Vegetable Stock
- 2 Cups Eggplant, Cubed
- 1 Tablespoon Coconut Oil

Directions:

1. Press sauté, and then melt your oil.
2. Put your eggplant cube sin first, cooking for two minutes.
3. Add in the stock and coconut milk, stirring well.
4. Throw in the seasoning and spinach, and cook on high pressure for four minutes. Use a quick release before serving warm.

CHILI CORN

Serves: 2
Time: 10 Minutes

Ingredients:

- 1 Cup Water
- 2 Ears Corn, Shucked
- 2 Teaspoons Butter, Divided
- ½ Tablespoon Chili Powder, Divided
- Sea Salt & Black Pepper to Taste

Directions:

1. Pour the water into your instant pot, and then add your steamer basket with the corn in it.
2. Cook on high for three minutes, and finish with a quick release. Top with butter and seasoning before serving.

ROSEMARY POTATOES

Serves: 2

Time: 35 Minutes

Ingredients:

- 1 ½ Tablespoons Butter
- 4 Potatoes, Sliced
- 1 Cup Chicken Broth
- ½ Sprig Rosemary, Fresh & Chopped

Directions:

1. Melt your butter by using sauté, and then throw the potatoes in.
2. Cook for ten minutes, and then add the broth and rosemary.
3. Cook on high pressure for seven minutes, and then use a quick release. Serve warm.

EASY YELLOW PEAS

Serves: 2

Time: 35 Minutes

Ingredients:

- 1 Potato, Chopped
- 1 Tablespoon Butter
- 1 Clove Garlic, Crushed
- 1 Cup Yellow Peas, Split
- 2 Cups Vegetable Stock
- ½ Cup Onion, Chopped
- ½ Carrot, Sliced
- ½ Teaspoon Cayenne Pepper
- Pinch Sea Salt

Directions:

1. Press sauté and fry your onions for two minutes in melted butter.
2. Throw the remaining vegetables in, cooking for seven minutes. Season with salt and cayenne, and cook for another minute.
3. Pour in your vegetable stock, and then cook on high pressure for twenty-five minutes. Use a quick release.

BACON & BEANS

Serves: 2
Time: 1 Hour

Ingredients:

- 1 Ounce Dark Molasses
- ¾ Cup Water
- ¼ Teaspoon Dry Mustard
- ½ Cup Navy Beans, Soaked Overnight
- ½ Onion, Small & Chopped
- 2 Ounces Bacon, Chopped
- Pinch Sea Salt

Directions:

1. Throw all ingredients into your instant pot, stirring until they're well combined.
2. Cook on low for forty-five minutes.
3. Use a quick release after a natural release for ten minutes.

STEAMED ASPARAGUS

Serves: 2
Time: 10 Minutes

Ingredients:

- ¼ Teaspoon Garlic Powder
- ½ Tablespoon Onion, Diced
- 1 Tablespoon Olive Oil
- ½ lb. Asparagus, Trimmed
- 1 Cup Water
- Sea Salt to Taste

Directions:

1. Pour your water into the instant pot, and then arrange your asparagus on the rack. Drizzle with oil.
2. Sprinkle with salt and onion, and then seal the lid.
3. Press steam, and then cook for two minutes before using a quick release. Serve warm.

DESSERT RECIPES

CITRUS CUSTARD

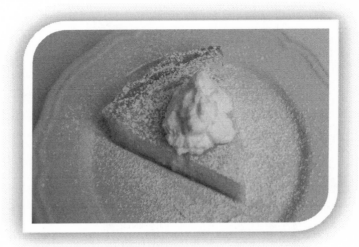

Serves: 2
Time: 50 Minutes (+2 Hours to Chill)

Ingredients:

- 2 Eggs, Large
- ½ Cup Sugar
- 1 Teaspoon Orange Zest, Grated Fine
- ½ Teaspoon Lemon Zest, Grated Fine
- ¼ Cup Orange Juice, Fresh
- ¼ Cup Lemon Juice, Fresh
- 2 Tablespoons Heavy Whipping Cream

Directions:

1. Start by getting a small bowl and whisk your sugar and eggs. Add in the zests, juices and cream. Whisk until smooth, and pour it into two ramekins.

2. Pour a cup of water into the instant pot, adding your trivet with the ramekins placed on top. Cover with foil loosely.

3. Cook on low pressure for six minutes, allowing for a natural release for ten minutes before finishing with a quick release.

4. Allow them to cool for twenty minutes to room temperature before cooling in the fridge for two hours before serving.

NUTMEG & MAPLE CUSTARD

Serves: 2

Time: 1 Hour 5 Minutes (+ 2 Hours to Chill)

Ingredients:

- 1 Cup Heavy Whipping Cream
- ½ Teaspoon Vanilla Extract, Pure
- Pinch sea Salt
- ½ Teaspoon Nutmeg, Grated Fresh
- 1 Tablespoon Brown Sugar
- ¼ Cup Maple syrup
- 1 Egg, Whole
- 2 Egg Yolks
- 1 Cup Heavy Whipping Cream

Directions:

1. Start by getting out a bowl and whisk your cream, egg yolks, and whole gg. Make sure it's well combined, and then whisk your brown sugar, salt, maple syrup, vanilla and nutmeg in next. Pour into two ramekins.

2. Put the trivet int eh pot with a cup of water. Put the ramekins on top with foil over them.

3. Cook on high pressure for eight minutes, and then use a natural release for ten minutes followed by a quick release.

4. Allow it to cool for twenty minutes before placing it in the fridge to chill for two hours before serving.

TAPIOCA PUDDING

Serves: 2
Time: 10 Minutes

Ingredients:

- ¼ Cup Sugar
- ¼ Teaspoon Vanilla Extract, Pure
- ¼ Cup Water
- ¼ Cup Tapioca Pearls
- ¼ Cup Sugar
- 1 Cup Almond Milk

Directions:

1. Start by adding the water in, and then get out a heatproof bowl. Put all remaining ingredients in the bowl, and mix well. Put the rack in, and place the bowl on it.
2. Cook on high pressure for eight minutes.
3. Allow for a natural pressure release for ten minutes, and serve warm or chilled.

EASY MANGO CAKE

Serves: 2
Time: 50 Minutes

Ingredients:

- 1 Cup Flour
- ½ Teaspoon Mango Syrup
- ½ Teaspoon Baking Powder
- 1/8 Cup Coconut Oil
- Sea Salt to Taste
- 1/8 Teaspoon Baking soda
- ½ Cup Milk
- 1 Cup Water
- ¼ Cup Sugar

Directions:

1. Start by greasing a pan using cooking spray, and add the water into your instant pot before placing n your trivet.

2. Get out a bowl and whisk all remaining ingredients.

3. Transfer this to your baking pan, and then set it on the trivet.

4. Cook on high pressure for thirty-five minutes. Use a quick release.

5. Refrigerate before serving.

RICOTTA CAKE WITH APPLES

Serves: 2
Time: 5 Minutes

Ingredients:

- 2 Apples, Dice One & Slice One

- 1/8 Cup Sugar

- ½ Cup Flour

- 1 Egg

- ½ Cup Ricotta

- 1 ½ Tablespoons Oil

- 1 Teaspoon Baking Powder

- ½ Teaspoon Baking Soda

- ½ Tablespoon Lemon Juice, Fresh

- ½ Teaspoon Vanilla Extract, Pure

Directions:

1. Pour two cups of water into the instant pot, and then get out a baking dish out. Line it with parchment paper, arranging your slices of apple on the bottom, and then sprinkle the lemon juice over the apple slices.

2. Get out a bowl out and whisk all remaining ingredients including the diced apple together to form a batter. Pour it over your apples. Put the pan inside the instant pot on at rivet.

3. Cook on high pressure for twenty minutes, and use a quick release.

EASY BROWNIES

Serves: 2
Time: 45 Minutes

Ingredients:

- 1/8 Cup Cocoa Powder
- ½ Cup Flour
- 1 Egg
- ½ Teaspoon Baking Powder
- 1/8 Teaspoon Salt
- ½ Cup Sugar
- ½ Tablespoon Honey, Raw
- ¼ Cup Butter, Melted

Directions:

1. Start by pouring a cup of water into the instant pot, and then mix all ingredients in a bowl.
2. Grease a pan using cooking spray before pouring the batter in. place it on a trivet, and cook on high pressure for thirty-five minutes. Use a quick release before serving.

LEMON MOUSSE

Serves: 2
Time: 45 Minutes (2 Hours to Chill)

Ingredients:

- 1/3 Cup + 2 Teaspoons Sugar
- 2 Tablespoons Butter, Unsalted & Room Temperature
- 2 Egg Yolks, Large
- 1 Lemon, Zested
- 3 Tablespoons Lemon Juice, Fresh
- ½ Cup Heavy Whipping Cream
- Pinch Sea Salt

Directions:

1. Take out a heatproof bowl, and make sure it fits into the instant pot. Beat your butter and sugar until the sugar is almost completely dissolved. Your mixture should be fluffy and light. Add in your egg yolk, beating until it's combined.

2. Add the lemon juice and lemon zest next, and then eat to combine. The mixture should turn grainy before covering the bowl with foil.

3. Add a cup of water to your inner pot, and then put a trivet in. put the bowl on top, and lock your lid.

4. Cook on high pressure for ten minutes, and then use a natural pressure release for ten more minutes before finishing with a quick release.

5. Discard the foil, and it should look like it's curdled some. Whisk well and then use a fine mesh strainer, and then press down so that the curds pass through. This will leave curdled egg bits and zest behind, which you will discard. Cover in plastic wrap, which will keep it from forming a skin, and allow it to cool for two hours in the fridge.

6. Whip your cream until it forms peaks, and then add 1/3 of it into the curd, folding it gently. Repeat with another 1/3, and then with the final cream serve it over the lemon mousse.

SPICED PEACH BREAD PUDDING

Serves: 2
Time: 40 Minutes

Ingredients:

- 1 Tablespoon Butter, Unsalted & Melted

- 3 Teaspoons Brown Sugar, Divided

- 1 Egg, Large

- 2/3 Cup Whole Milk

- ¼ Teaspoon Vanilla Extract, Pure

- Pinch Sea Salt

- ½ Teaspoon Cinnamon

- ¼ Teaspoon Cardamom

- 2 Cups Pound Cake, Cubed

- ¼ Peaches, Frozen, Thawed & Chopped

Directions:

1. Start by getting out two custard cups that will hold one cup each or ramekins. Brush the sides with the butter. Sprinkle a half a teaspoon of brown sugar into each one.

2. Get out a bowl and whisk the egg, vanilla, salt, cinnamon, cardamom, vanilla and milk. Add in your remaining two teaspoons of brown sugar and whisk well. Add the pound cake, and toss it into your egg mixture. Make sure it's well coated. Allow it to sit for three minutes to soak up the egg mixture, and then toss a few times to make sure that it's well distributed. Stir the peaches in.

3. Divide between cups, and add a cup of water to your instant pot before placing the trivet in. top with ramekins, and cover with foil. Lock the lid, and cook on high pressure for ten minutes.

4. Use a quick release, and allow them to cool for ten minutes before serving.

CONCLUSION

Now you have everything that you need to get started cooking with the instant pot for two people. You can say goodbye to the pressure to buy unhealthy food just so that you can have a good, quick meal. With the instant pot, your life just got easier. No reason to slave over the stove either. Just pick a recipe and follow it to see the magic that the instant pot can bring into your life. You'll be eating healthier and delighting your taste buds in no time. It's even perfect for a quick romantic dinner no matter how busy your day was. The instant pot is the future of cooking, and there's no reason that you shouldn't use it to your advantage.

Made in the USA
Middletown, DE
11 November 2019

78210570R00073